Frozen Worlds

Project Editor Allison Singer
Assistant Editor Prerna Grewal
Art Editors Emma Hobson, Mohd Zishan
Jacket Editor Francesca Young
Jacket Designers Amy Keast, Dheeraj Arora
DTP Designer Dheeraj Singh
Picture Researcher Sakshi Saluja
Producer, Pre-production Nadine King
Producer Niamh Tierney
Managing Editors Laura Gilbert, Monica Saigal
Managing Art Editors Diane Peyton Jones, Neha Ahuja Chowdhry
Art Director Martin Wilson
Publisher Sarah Larter
Publishing Director Sophie Mitchell

Reading Consultant
Jacqueline Harris

First published in Great Britain in 2017
by Dorling Kindersley Limited
80 Strand, London, WC2R 0RL

A CIP catalogue record for this book is available from the British Library.
ISBN: 978-0-2412-8504-6

Printed and bound in China

The publisher would like to thank the following for their kind permission to reproduce their photographs:
(Key: a-above; b-below/bottom; c-centre; f-far; l-left; r-right; t-top)
1 123RF.com: Anthony Lister. **3 123RF.com**: Eric Isselee (br). **4–5 PunchStock**: Digital Vision / Tim Hibo (b).
6–7 Getty Images: Jeff Schultz / Design Pics. **7 Alamy Stock Photo**: Blickwinkel (cb). **8–9 Alamy Stock Photo**: Steve
Davey Photography. **10–11 123RF.com**: Roman Babakin (t). **11 Robert Harding Picture Library**: Christian Goupi (cb).
12–13 Courtesy of the National Science Foundation: Julian Race, NSF. **14–15 Courtesy of the National Science
Foundation**: Dave Munroe. **15 123RF.com**: Richard Lindie (ca). **16–17 Courtesy of the National Science Foundation**:
Peter Rejcek. **17 Courtesy of the National Science Foundation**: Emily Stone, NSF (cb). **18–19 iStockphoto.com**:
Heckepics. **19 Courtesy of the National Science Foundation**: Jeff Keller (c).b**20–21 123RF.com**: Witold Kaszkin (t).
22 123RF.com: Anatoli Kosolapov (bl); Eric Isselee (cl); Gigra (clb).

Jacket images: *Front:* **123RF.com**: Kongsak Sumano tc, Lynn Bystrom ca; **Dreamstime.com**: Mythja (Background);
Getty Images: Altrendo Images b; *Back:* **123RF.com**: Eric Isselee tl

Endpaper Images: *Front:* **Courtesy of the National Science Foundation:** Laura Gerwin;
Back: **Courtesy of the National Science Foundation:** Laura Gerwin

Contents

The Arctic

The Arctic
is a very cold place.
Brrr!

It is at the top
of the Earth.
The Arctic Ocean
is full of ice.

Arctic

Life in the Arctic

These children
live in the Arctic.
They dress warmly
to play in the snow.

Polar bears

Polar bears live
in the Arctic, too.
These furry animals
like to eat fish.

On the move

A reindeer pulls a sleigh
across the snow.

10

Zoom!
Here comes a snowmobile.

The Antarctic

The Antarctic is at the bottom of the Earth.

It is even colder than the Arctic!

Antarctic

Icebergs

Big icebergs float
in the sea.
The icebergs melt.
Drip, drip.

Penguins

Emperor penguins
live in the Antarctic.

They swim in
the cold sea and
look for fish to eat.

Sea animals

Splash!
A whale leaps out
of the water.

A seal watches
from the rocks.

Light show

Sometimes the night sky
lights up in many colours.

What an amazing sight!

Glossary

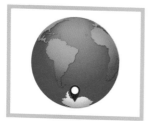

Antarctic
cold place at the
bottom of the Earth

Arctic
cold place at the
top of the Earth

fur
soft hair that covers
the skin of some animals

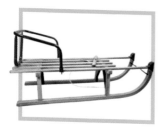

sleigh
wagon that is pulled
by an animal over snow

snowmobile
machine that travels
over snow and ice

Index

A Note to Parents

DK Readers is a four-level interactive reading adventure series for children, developing the habit of reading widely for both pleasure and information.

Beautiful illustrations and superb full-colour photographs combine with engaging, easy-to-read narratives to offer a fresh approach to each subject in the series. Each DK Reader is guaranteed to capture a child's interest while developing his or her reading skills, general knowledge and love of reading.

The four levels of DK Readers are aimed at different reading abilities, enabling you to choose the books that are exactly right for your child:

Level 1: Learning to read
Level 2: Beginning to read
Level 3: Beginning to read alone
Level 4: Reading alone

The "normal" age at which a child begins to read can be anywhere from three to eight years old. Adult participation through the lower levels is very helpful for providing encouragement, discussing storylines and sounding out unfamiliar words.

No matter which level you select, you can be sure that you are helping your child learn to read, then read to learn!